Investing and Trading for Novices

By John Huberman MD

Table of Contents:

Chapter 1. Forward to Investing and Trading for novices

I am an 85 year old retired physician who knew nothing about finance until I was in my 30's and was able to start saving some money. I decided to learn something about investing so that I could manage my own finances and my retirement savings. When I retired in my mid-sixties and had more time on my hand's I started trading ETFs and stocks. Over time I read a lot of books and articles, made a lot of mistakes, and learned a few things.

When I started writing this book it was with the thought of passing on what I had learned about investing and trading to my children and grandchildren, but as the book progressed it became apparent that it could be of value to a much wider audience of novice investors and traders. The purpose of this book is to pass what I have learned that works and is useful from a non-professional investor and trader's point of view, that helps reduce the mistakes one makes in learning a new skill, and that gives a novice some confidence in navigating the management of their investments and their ability to trade.

This represents my personal views but it is the responsibility of the reader to utilize what he or she feels is of value and discard what they disagree with.

John Huberman MD

Chapter 2.   Investing and Trading for Novices

Via my experience in trying to learn how to invest and trade, my readings in finance, and my mistakes, I have tried to distill what I learned that has worked for me into a relatively concise discourse presented here. There is much noise, hysteria, nonsense and risk that one must confront in investing and trading. There are so many different venues (stocks, bonds, stock etfs, bond etfs, mutual funds, options, futures, currencies, commodities, etc). This can become overwhelming to a novice investor and trader. This discourse is meant to provide novices with relatively conservative strategies to help them function in this arena without having to pay the price of learning everything on their own. Most books dealing with this subject are written by professionals in the field. I am not a professional, I am a retired physician, and this discourse presents what a non-professional has found to be important and useful in learning how to invest and trade. I believe this point of view may be of value to novices and even to non-novices.

To learn a skill one must start out simply. We will not deal with trading options, futures, currencies, leveraged etfs, or selling short, and we mainly invest in US ETFs, Bonds, and US stocks.

Before starting to invest or trade there are some basics that the novice needs to learn:

1. a basic understanding of "Financial Instruments"

2. a basic understanding of "Economics", "Inflation", and "Interest Rates"

3. a basic understanding of "Technical(Visual) Analysis"

4. Identifying the "Market Regime"(see below)

5. having a "trading platform"

6. having a secure financial institution(brokerage) to hold your investments, trades,cash, IRAs, etc.

7. having a "mentor"

There are many introductory books on the above subjects available on Amazon, in the " Chart School" section of Stockcharts.com(see below), on Investopedia and Wikipedia, on Youtube(videos), and by looking up any term or subject in search on your web browser or in AI(artificial intelligence) platform like CoPilot on Windows or the AI platform on Googl. I will now present some thoughts on the basics of Techinical Analysis and identifying the Market Regime.

"Technical Analysis" is the "visual analysis of price charts " in various time frames, and the visual interpretation of derivatives of price(indicators). Price can be indicated on a chart by the closing price with a line, or by the high, low, open and close with a candlestick, or by the high, low and close with a bar. Overlays like moving averages and various indicators which are all derivatives of price, can be added to the chart. The "trend" of the trade, the direction of price movement in time, is either an "uptrend"—a succession of price movements characterized by higher highs and higher lows, or a "downtrend"—a succession of price movements characterized by lower highs and lower lows, or non-trending—a horizontal movement of price within a range.

Support and Resistance levels are price levels at which further movement of price above or below the level can be challenging. Common resistance levels are recent highs or previous highs, moving averages, upper and lower Keltner channels, upper and lower Bollinger bands, and Ichimoku Cloud tops and bottoms. Common support levels are recent lows, previous lows, the low on a gap up and the high the day before, moving averages, the upper and lower Keltner channel, the upper and lower Bollinger bands, and the Ichimoku Cloud tops and bottoms. After support or resistance is bypassed by price the previous resistance level now becomes support if the price starts falling, and the previous support level now becomes resistance if the price starts rising.

Market Breadth is another important aspect of technical analysis. For the market to be really healthy then a majority of the industries in the SP500 should be advancing in price, and a majority of the stocks in a given industry should be advancing in price. In other words the advance in the "market" should not be limited to a few stocks like the Mags(Apple,Nvidia,Amazon,Google, Tesla, Meta,Microsoft,NFLX) but should be distributed more evenly, and in addition to large caps advancing the mid caps and small caps should also be participating in the advance.

To gauge "Market Breadth" one can use a broad index like the $NYA index(the NY stock exchange) which includes most of the stocks traded on the NY stock exchange. I use the following list of indicators to gauge market breadth:

      1. !ADLINENYC the NYSE common stock only advance-decline cumulative

2. the $BPNYA the percent of stocks in the $NYA showing buy signals on the point and figure charts.

3. the $NYA100R the percent of stocks in the $NYA above the sma(100,daily close)

4. $NYHILO and $NYHL(area) the percent of stocks in the $NYA with new highs -new lows.

5. $NYMO the McClellan oscillator which is an indicator of market breadth and displays positive market breadth when it is above the 0 line.

6. the $NYSI the NYSE McClellan summation index which is a cumulative display of the McClellan oscillator and displays positive market breadth when it is above 0.

These indicators can all be found and explained in more detail in the Stock Charts school. They basically gauge the percent of participation of all the stocks in the NYA index in an adance or decline in the market.

As mentioned above the indicators used in technical analysis are all derived from price and can help in interpreting price movement and the momentum of price action. The "Chart School" section in Stockcharts.com is an excellent source of help here and has excellent, informative, discourses on all the important indictors and their derivatives.To invest and trade you need to achieve a basic understanding of the visual analysis of price charts and indicators. Don't proceed until you have accomplished this. There are many different indicators and some of them are complex in their derivation. What's important with indicators is to learn what they signify and how to use them. Don't worry about trying to remember exactly how they were derived.

Most of my chart analysis involves looking at a daily or weekly chart with price represented by candlesticks, a few moving averages of price, the Ichimoku Cloud, and Keltner Channels. On the daily chart I use the 5 day sma, 25 day ema, 50 day sma, 105 day ema, and the 200 day sma moving average of price, the Ichimoku Cloud(9,26,52), Keltner Channels(105,3.0,30),the daily PPO line(12,2,6,9), the daily RSI(14), daily SCTR line,daily Volume, daily Chaikin Money flow (20), and the daily AccDist line with a 50 day moving average. Price is either represente by candlesticks or by solid thick black line. Trend determination is visual by noting successions of higher highs and higher lows(an uptrend), lower highs and lower lows(a downtrend), or non-trending(horizontal price action within a range), the "slope of the Keltner Channel and Ichimoku Cloud, and the slope of the 25 day,50 day 105 day and 200 day moving averages.

On the weekly charts I use price represent by candlesticks or by a solid thick black line, 10 week, 21 week, and 40 week moving averages, a weekly Keltner Channel(21,1.0,20),the weekly Ichimoku Cloud(9,26,52), the weekly a PPO line(12,26,9), a weekly RSI(14), weekly Chaikin Moneyflow(20), and weekly Accumulation/Distribultion line with a 25 week moving average(read about these indicators in Stockcharts.com "Chart School").

An excellent free article on technical analysis is John Murphy"s 'Charting made easy e-book" available on Stockcharts "articles, John Murphy" or in the search symbol on Stockcharts.com

"The US stock market"(the market) can be represented by the SP500 index($SPX) or SPY. The SP500 index is a broad,diversified, cap weighted, large cap index of US stocks that serves as a bell-weather for the entire US stock market. It is made up of the largest 500 cap weighted stocks (stock price x number of outstanding shares) that meet certain standards set by the Standard and Poor's Index committees. The 500 stocks are then identified by the industry and sector they are in, the sector percentage is determined by the (number of stocks in that given sector / 500). Currently in June 2023 the sector percentages are as follows:

Technology   26.4%, Communication Services 8.3%, Consumer Discretionary 10.2%, Industrials 8.2%, Financial Services 12.6%, Healthcare 14.5%, Materials 2.4%, Consumer Staples 7.3%, Energy 4.7%, Real Estate 2.6%, Utilities 2.9.

Each sector is comprised of the industries that fall into that sector and all the industries are represented by stocks that comprise the SP500 index. Thus, when you hold the SP500 index, you hold a group of large cap stocks representing all the sectors and industries in those sectors. The exchange traded fund SPY is comprised of all the stocks in the SP500 index, and is used by finance and trading professionals to represent the stock market. So by evaluating the chart for SPY or $SPX one can infer how the entire stock market if faring. Another broader stock index is $NYA (the NYequity only stock exchange). It should be noted that several stocks comprise a signficant percentage of the total value of the SP500. These include AAPL,GOOGL,NVDA,MSFT,NFLX,TSLA,META. Therefore the behavior of these 7 stocks have a significant effect on the behavior of the entire stock market, and when one is constructing an investment portfolio they should include other stock etfs that have less weighting in the above 7 stocks.

"The Market Regime" identifies the health and state of the "the market". It can be in one of three states. When it is "bullish" SPY is in an uptrend, its price is moving higher, it is making a series of higher highs and higher lows, most of the sectors and industries comprising SPY are moving higher, market breadth(the percentage stocks participating in the uprend) is high, long term interest rates are falling or below 4%, investors are optimistic, and the economy is robust. When it is "bearish" SPY in a downtrend, its price is moving lower, it is making a series of lower highs and lower lows or moving horizontally, most of the sectors and industries comprising Spy are moving lower, long term interest rates are rising or above 4%, investors are pessimistic, and the economy is faltering or has entered a recession. The price action of most stocks are highly correlated to the price action of SPY(the market), and therefore one can use the price action of SPY to represent the market regime. When it is trendless Spy is moving horizontally within the Keltner Channel, and the Keltner Channel bcomes horizontal.

When the "Market Regime" is bullish one wants to be fully invested in stock etfs, stocks, or both, and be trading. When the "Market Regime" is trendless or bearish one wants to reduce their exposure to stock etfs, stocks, and move money into cash or other safe havens(eg bonds, gold), and one wants to stop trading. So it is important to identify when the "Market Regime" becomes bullish or bearish. This is not as easy as one may think. I have a list of 35 indicators that reflect on the market regime. For the market regime to be declared bearish most of these indicators must turn bearish. For the market regime to be termed bullish most of these indicators must turn bullish .This is too cumbersome and time consuming for a novice investor and trader. I have found that by using my weekly chart for SPY(see above for the parameters) when price(represented by the weekly solid, thick black line) crosses from above the upper weekly Keltner Channel(21,1.50,20) to below the lower weekly Keltner Channel, or below the sma(40,weekly close), whichever comes first, and the upper weekly Keltner Channel is above the weekly Ichimoku Cloud Top, this corresponds well to when most of the 35 indicators turn bearish and the market regime can be considered to be bearish. For the market regime to change from bearish to bullish, the weekly close for SPY must cross from below the lower Keltner Channel(21,1.50,20) to above the upper Keltner Channel, and the upper Keltner Channel must be above the Ichimoku Cloud Top. The weekly close must penetrate the upper Keltner Channel. When this occurs most of the 35 market regime indicators have turned bullish. When the market regime is trendless, Spy is moving horizontally within the Keltner Channel for an extended period of time.Thus with a glance at my weekly chart for SPY(the market), one can tell whether the market regime is bullish, bearish, or trendless.

The same holds for the daily chart for SPY. When the daily close is above the upper daily Keltner Channel(105,3.0,30) and the daily upper Kelt chan is above the daily Ichimoku Cloud and sloping up, the market regime is bulllish.When the daily close falls below the 200 day sma or below the lower daily Keltner channel(which ever comes first) the market regime is bearish.

When price is within the Keltner channel the market regime is in a transitional phase from bullish to bearish, or bearish to bullish. If it continues falling it could reach bear market status, if it reverses and starts rising, and crosses above the upper Kelt. Chan. you are back in a bullish regime. If it stays within the Keltner Channnel and starts moving horizontally for an extended period of time, and the Keltner Channel also moves horizontally your are in a trendless situation and the market regime is neither bullish or bearish.

This is easier and less time consuming than checking 35 indicators, and it represent very useful information for a novice. You must remember the above to be able to tell if the market regime is bullish, bearish, or trendless.

To invest and trade one needs a "trading platform ". I use Stockcharts.com. There are many other trading platforms but this is the one I started with and the only one I have extensive experience with. For novices its chart school, blogs, plugins, charting, indicators and scan engine are excellent. Its contributors like Dave Keller, Tom Bowley, Jayanthi, and MAry McGonicle are excellent. I think it is the best trading platform for novices, has an easy to learn and use scanning engine, and its fees are reasonable. The Stockcharts scanning engine is one way to rapidly identify top sectors, industries and stocks.

One also must have a secure financial institution(brokerage) to hold your investments and conduct your trades. I use Fidelity and am very pleased with them. There are others like Schwab that are also excellent. I recommend you stick to one of the major financial institutions to hold your investments, conduct your trades, keep your financial records, and provide you with income tax information.

Chapter 3. Investing

Investing is purchasing financial instruments for the long term with the purpose of building a retirement fund to support you when you stop working, or having a financial cushion behind you so if unexpected expenses arise you don't get wiped out and thrown into a financial crisis, or providing for your children's educational expenses, or putting your savings to work so that they grow in amount and increase your level of wealth.

For novice investors I recommend their activities be limited to learning how to manage their investment accounts in IRAs, Roth IRAs, or personal-non-IRA investment accounts. If you are working and earning income ideally all your investment accounts would be in IRAs or Roth IRAs because of their significant tax advantages. In regular(simple) IRAs you can contribute pre-tax dollars to the IRA which reduces your taxable income, In Roth IRAs and personal non-IRA investment accounts you can only contribute after tax dollars. Once money is in an IRA(either simple or Roth) it can grow tax free until you start taking distributions from it later on in life which are then taxed as income if they re generated by a simple IRA, however they are not taxes if generated by a Roth IRA. Any interest,dividends or capital gains generated in the IRAs are not taxed, and these monies reinvested in the IRA allow it to compound tax free, resulting in significant growth of the IRA over a lifetime. The net result is IRAs allow you to reap the benefits of tax free compounding of your investment over time. You can trade in the IRAs and any capital gains will not be taxed when you sell the trade. In contrast after tax dollars contributed to a non-IRA investment account will have any interest or dividends taxed in the year they are generated, and any capital gains from sales of trades taxed also in the year they were generated, so the growth of a non-IRA investment account cannot match the growth of an IRA over time because of this taxation. The only reason to open a non-IRA investment account is if you max out your allowable yearly contributions to your IRA and Roth IRA, and still have investable income available.

The only investments I make in my IRAs and Non-IRA investment account are bond etfs, stock etfs, cash, and short term Treasury notes. I prefer using ETFs rather than mutual funds for these investments because they have lower fees, can be bought or sold at any time without any restrictions, usually don't generate any unexpected capital gains, have mostly index generated holdings, and are not actively managed in general. I dont usuallly invest in any foreign etfs as most of the time the foreign etfs underperform US etfs. However when the US Dollar is weak and falling, then foreign etfs start to outperform US etfs and I will consider adding them to my investment accounts.

The composition of my investment portfolios was initially 75%stock etfs and 25% bond etfs until I reached the age of 50. At that age I reduced the stock etf portion by 2%/year and invested that 2% in bond etfs so that by the time I was 65 the portfolio was 50% stock etfs and 50% bond etfs. When you retire you need cash and the bond etf portion of your portfolio supplies that cash. When you rebalance the stock etf and bond etf portions this involves selling and capital gains generation. However in an IRA any capital gains generated are not taxed so you dont have to worry about that.. All interest,dividends and capital gains should be automatically reinvested in the etf generating them until you retire to achieve maximum growth of the portfolio. After you retire you must capture any interest and dividends to provide you with cash to live on.

In the stock portion of the my investment portfolios I keep 50% of the monies in SPY and the other 50% in large cap blend etfs that have different sector representation from SPY (usually more conservative) like: MOAT,FNDX,FDL,OEF,PKW,QUAL,RWL,SPHQ,RSP,SPLV,SPMO,USMV,VIG, SPHD, SCHD and BRK/B. (see my chartlist ETFs traded in my investment accounts)

In the bond portion of the portfolio besides true bond etfs I include stock etfs that specialize in generating high dividends.Thus in actuality the total stock portion of my portfolios is higher than stated. The distinction of bonds is further blurred by the fact that some of these high yielding etfs are covered call etfs, convertibles, and preferred stock etfs, which are related more to stocks than they are to bonds. I try to find true "bond etfs" that are generating at least a yield of 3% or greater. Some of the "bonds" I hold are:

BIZD,BKLN,EPP,HDV,HYG,HYS,JEPI,JEPQ,LQD,MDIV,PEY,PFF,SRLN,TOTL,USHY, VCIT,VRP,VWEHX,DVY,HYLS,SHYG,SCHD,VYM,VCIT,BND

If long term individual treasury bonds like the 10 or 20 yr bonds are yielding over 4% I might also purchase them also as they a "risk" free investments and hold them to maturity.

The purpose of the bond portion of the portfolio is to provide a steady stream of interest and dividends that when automatically reinvested contribute to the "magic" of compound interest which over time can lead to significant growth of the portfolio, and in retirement to provide income. Having "bonds" in the portfoilio also is a good diversifier and helps reduce he drawdowns that occur when the "market " is bearish.

I dont trade or sell any of the bond etfs or treasury bonds, and I dont trade or sell any of the stock etfs I hold except for SPY(see below). These are always long term buy and hold investments. In retirement both the bond and stock portions of the portfolio will generate dividends. These dividends are invested in short term treasury notes, and at the end of the year these notes are all sold and converted to cash that now makes up part of your yearly RMD(required minimum distribution from your retirement accounts), and income from your non-IRA accounts if you have them.

The purpose of the stock portion of the portfolio is to provide long term growth. I personally will trade up to 25% of the stock etf portion in SPY. This amounts to 12.5% of the entire stock etf portfolio as SPY comprises 50% of the stock etf portfolio. I will also trade the other 75% of the stock portion in SPY if the market regime becomes bearish. I never trade the other 50%of non Spy equities and the "bond" portion of the portfolio.These are buy and hold.

Depending on the time you have available to manage your investment portfolio and your experience in trading you can choose one of the following methods to manage the investment portfolio:

1. Simply buy and hold.

All you do here is invest your yearly IRA contribution in your stock and bond etfs, and rebalance the portfolio once a year to the appropriate stock and bond etf percentages, and reinvest any dividends and capital gains automatically.You dont trade anything.

2. Buy and hold with addition of capital preservation(hedging)

Here, if on the weekly chart for SPY the weekly close crosses below the 21 week ema(105 day ema) you sell 25% of you position in Spy and hold the proceeds in cash. If the weekly close for SPY now drops below the 30 week(150 day ema) ema you sell another 25% of your position in SPY and add it to cash. If it now drops below the 40 week sma(200 day sma or the lower weekly Kelt Chan(21,1.50,20), whichever comes first on the chart, and the upper Keltner Channel is above the Ichimoku Cloud Top(you now have a bearish market regime) you sell the remaining 50% of your position in SPY and place that in cash. When the market bottoms you reinvest the cash in SPY.(see chapter on Hedging and Capital preservation). So basically you are only trading SPY in this scenario.

3 . Trading up to 25% of your position in SPY in other ETFs that are outperforming SPY in addition to capital preservation.

I limit my trading of etfs in the investment account to US etfs that are outperforming the "market", however if foreign etfs are outperforming US etffs I will also inlcude some of them.. These can be growth etfs,,value etfs,,blend etfs,commodity etfs,gold and silver etfs,Sector etfs, and SubSector etfs,small and mid cap etfs.

In the growth category I included etfs like MAGS,SPYG,FBCG, QQQ,SMH,SPMO,XLK,VUG,IUSG,and MGC, AIQ, and Ives. When you have a strong bullish market regime you want to have excess representation in in growth stocks. However the market regime can remain bullish, but due to Sector Rotation the outperforming etfs can change. Thus one must quarterly review my chartlist "ETFs traded in my investment account" which includes all the growth, value, blend, gold, commodities, Sector   and SubSector,Mkt Cap Style etfs in "Summary" form with a three month timespan and ranked by [daily pctrelative(66,SPY)] to see which of these are the top etfs that are outperforming SPY currently. Then you adjust your traded etf holdings in the investment account accordingly.

You trade up to 25% of your holdings in SPY in the above ETFS that are outperforming SPY(the market) and try to hold them thru the entire quarter. Depending on what you can afford you invest anywhere from $500 to $5,000 in each trade, and if the start doing well(5% gain or better in the first few weeks) you increase the amount by another $500 to $5,000 for a max investment of $10,000 in each etf.

So in this scenario you are trading both SPY and other ETFs that were outperforming the market (SPY).

In retirement you stop reinvesting all the interest and dividends from your stock and bond portfolios in both your IRAs and non-IRA investment accounts and capture them to provide you with the income you need in your retirement. If you have income or capital gains from trading in a a non-IRA investment account you must remember to set aside some of your gains for taxes. I determine the amount to set aside by total Fed and State taxes paid last year/ total income on my federal return.(see chapter on taxes).

I rarely trade foreign stock ETFs.I just concentrate on US stock etfs. Most of the time foreign stock etfs underperform the US market(SPY), and trying to deal with the US market is enough of a challenge without adding foreign markets. However if foreign stock etfs are significantly outperforming the US marekt(SPY) I will trade them. I don't trade mid- cap and small- cap etfs unless they are outperforming SPY and interest rates are low or dropping. Most of the time they underperform the "market". In the investment accounts I try to trade the above etfs on a quarterly basis(see below), sell them at the end of a quarter(see below), and start the new quarter with the current etfs that are outperforming SPY.

Chapter 4. Trading

I have around 5% of my the entire stock portion of my portfolio in a separate trading account in which I trade stocks that are outperforming the market, and I will trade up to 25% of my total position in SPY in my investments accounts in ETFs that are outperforming the market. The purpose here is to select the top stocks and etfs at the beginning of a trading quarter and try to hold them thru the entire quarter and thru their earnings report if they are stocks. You have to guard against "overtrading" here. From my experience "overtrading" is a loosing proposition.

I am a "trend" trader. I like to enter trades that are in a strong, established uptrend and try to hold them thru the entire quarter. My scans and charts are all designed around this principle. Another way to trade is to try and enter a trade much earlier when it starts reversing from a downtrend and switches over from lower lows and lower highs to higher lows and higher highs. This is a valid method also, but my preference is to enter a trade later when it is in a more established uptrend.

For me to enter an intermediate term quarterly trade the trade must display the following characteristics:

1. the daily close must be above the 25 day ema.

2. the daily close must be above the upper daily Kelt Chan(105,3.0,30)

3. the upper Kelt Chan must be above the Ichimoku Cloud Top

4. the daily RSI(14) must be above 50, the daily PPO line(12,26,9,daily close) must be at or above 0, the SCTR must be at or above 60]

5. the weekly ROC(25)-the 6 mo ROC must be above 10.

the weekly ROC(12) - the 3 mo ROC must be above 5

the weekly ROC(4) - the one month ROC must be avoe 1.66

and the weekly ROC(1) - the one week ROC must be above 0.

6. The trade must meet the Keller requirements for a poistive intermediate term trend:

the weekly PPO(1,5,0) > 0]

the weekly PPO(5,13,0) > 0

the weekly PPO(21,34,0) > 0

see description of the Keller requirements below)

7. the ema(25,daily close) > sma(50,daily close)

the sma(50,daily close) > ema(105,daily close)

the ema(105,daily close > sma(200,daily close)

8. the "market regime" must be bullish, and the "Permission to trade long scan" should be positive

19. the trade should be outperforming the "market(SPY) over a 6 mo period by 5% assuming that in a bullish market regime the 6 mo ROC for SPY is 5%

thus weekly ROC(25) -6 mo >= 10%

weekly ROC(5)-3 mo >= 5%

weekly ROC(4) -1 mo >= 1.66%

weekly ROC(1)-1 week >= 0]

10. Ideally for a stock trade it should be in a top industry and outperforming the market, its industry, and the industry should be outperforming the market.

11. From a fundamental evaluation standpoint of a trade, I just require that the trade beat its earnings estimate and revenues estimate in the past quarter. This is a must, and it must be both earnings and revenues to be considered a candidate. Tom Bowley of EarningsBeats.com has done the research to show how important this factor is.

12. I enter these trades immediately at the beginning of a new quarter. I dont wait for a significant pullback to enter a trade as this takes too much observation becomes impractical when you a doing multiple trades.

The above requirements incorporate a "momentum" strategy. Momentum is the tendency of a trade that has been in an uptrend for 6 months or longer to maintain that uptrend and price rise over the next 3 months. I also incorporates Dave Kellers(my mentor) intermediate term uptrend ranking system. It requires the trade to be outperforming the marekt (SPY), and it requires that the 25 day ema, 50 day sma, 105 day em and 200day sma be positioned relative to each other in an uptrend fashion. It aslo requires the "market" to be bullish, and the trade to be preferably in a leading industry, and havestrong fundamentals with both earnings and revenues beating the estimatesfor the quarter.

Entering a trade is pretty straight forward. Exiting a trade is another matter. Remember, you are entering trades that are in strong uptrends and trying to hold them throughout the entire quarter(see chapter on quarterly method of trading). Unfortunately it may not be possible to hold a trade for the entire quarter if its uptrend starts deteriorating and the trade starts loosing money. I have investigated and tried numerous ways, numerous indicators,numerous chart styles, relative strength charts, etc. etc. to decide when to exit a trade. It is not easy. You have to balance not overtrading with exit signals, and not exiting a trade when you should have really remained it the trade.

The exit system I have finally adopted satisfies achieving a balance for me. Its not perfect but it works well most of the time. When you are exiting trades you have to be decisive, otherwise small losses will mushroom into large losses. I will exit a trade if either of 4 technical conditions are met:

1. if the sma(2,daily close) < sma(50,daily close), and the daily RSI(14) < 40 (both must be present)

or 2. if the sma(2,daily close) < daily upper Keltner Channel(105,3.0,30), and the daily RSI(14) < 40 (both must be present)

or 3. if the [daily sma(2,ROC(50)) < 3.50]

If the daily sma(2)of the ROC(50) falls below 3.50 that can be a strong indication to exit a trade.

4. If the sma(2,daily close) crossses below the "best fit moving average + 5 " fit to the lows of the sma(2) daily close over the past 2 months, in a bullish market regime, of it crosses below the best fit moving average +2 in a bearish market regime.

After studying the charts for many trades that I exited, I realized that using the above criteria for exiting achieved the balance for me of not overtrading with exit signals I was looking for. I have a scan for exiting trades that incorporates the above which I run daily. If a trade appears on the scan I look at the it's chart, and I will exit that trade over 90% of the time.

Conditions 1 and 2 get you out of trades a bit late with moderate losses. Condition 3 gets you out of a trade earlier. Condition 4 gets you out earlier and is the exit criteria I use on most of my trades.I will also confirm it by looking at condition 3. If you just use the "best fit moving average" crossover to exit you are exiting at the end of a rally and I find you are overtrading. However by adding 5 points to the "best fit moving average" you are giving the trade some "breathing room" and I find doing this helps achieve the balance between overtrading with exit signals.

I have a chartstyle labeled "chart for exiting current stock and etf trades".

1 year duration daily chart with

sma(2,daily close) as solid line

daily Kelt Chan(105,3.0,30)

daily Ichimoku Cloud

daily ema(50,daily close)

daily sma(2,RSI(14)) above with horizontal lines at 40 and 60

daily sma(2,ROC(50)) below with horizontal line at 3.50

I use the ema(50) not the sma(50 because I find it makes determining the best fit moving average easier and more accurate. I move the ema(50) up and down in value until I get a best fit moving average to the lows on the sma(2,daily close) and then add 5 points to the best fit moving average. Eg. if the best fit moving average is 18 then I use 18 + 5 = 23 as the exit best fit moving average, and exit the trade if the sma(2,daily close) crosses below 23.

I place all my trades in the current stock trade chartlist and current etf trade chartlist in the above chartstyle form and when I enter the trade I determine the best fit moving average plus 5 and use that. If the sma(2) daily close crosses below the best fit moving average + 5 I bring up the full chart of the trade and study it. Remember:

If the market regime is bullish; if the permission to trade long scan is positive; if the sm(2,daily close is at or above the sma(50,daily close); if the slope of the sma(50) daily close, sma(105) daily close,sma(200) daily close are up; if the sma(2,daily close) is above the upper Keltner Channel; if the moving averages are in the proper order (25 day ema > to day sma, 50 day sma > 105 day ema, and the 105 day ema > 200 day sma; if the daily RSI(14) >= 40; if the slope of the Kelt Chan and the Ichimoku Cloud are up; and the current Ichimoku Cloud is green; then you can stay in the trade and that would negate the sma(2,daily close) crossover with the best fit moving average + 5.

I find i can run thru the exit charts for all my trades daily (on average about 60 trades) in less than 10 minutes after the market closes or the next morning before it opens and determine if any trade needs to be exited. Another way to do this would be to set an alert for each trade on the Stockcharts Alert system for when the sma(2,daily close) of a trade crosses the "best fit moving average + 5 " for the trade.

Note is the market regime becomes bearish I exit if the trade crosses the best fit moving average + 2.

There are other reasons to exit a trade:

1. if the trade gets downgraded by a respected analyst

2. if the trade fails to beat earnings or revenues estimates on its earnings report

3.. if the trade develops strong bearish candlestick patterns such as a bearish engulfing pattern, a head and shoulder pattern, a double top, 3 black crows, or if it breakouts below a channel

4. to collect a large profit before the quarter ends.

5. if the sma(2,daily close) of SPY(the "market") closes below the ema(105,daily close) in the Keltner Channel(105,3.0,30) I will sell all my stock trades immediately.

6. If the market regime turns bearish.

When I started out trading I didn't have the above knowledge and was overtrading and getting into trouble, and causing a lot of anxiety for myself. Over several years I arrived at the above criteria for exiting a trade, and that has made me a better trader, saved me lots of time, and allowed me to face the "market" with much more tranquility.

There are thousands of etfs and stocks, and over 100 industries. How does one select the top etfs sectors, top etf subsectors, top industries and top stocks from these thousands. One has to develop a process for handling all the above data to achieve the desired end, the identification of the current top etfs, top industries, and top stocks in those industries that are outperforming the market and are in established, sustainable uptrends. The goal of trading is to make money by buying and selling etfs or stocks in strong uptrends that are outperforming the "market"(SPY) and hold them thru a quarter if possible. When a trade is outperforming the "market" it is said to possess "Relative Strength".

Relative strength measures the change in price of one entity relative to another. If A is a stock and B is Spy(the market) and if A has a value of 2 on a given date and B has a value of 10 on that date, and a week later A has a value of 6 and B has a value of 20, then the relative strength of A to B on day one is 2/10 = 0.20 , and the relative strength of A to B at the weeks end is 6/20 = 0.30. If you plot these values on a chart you will see that the relative strength of A is increasing relative to B, and that A is outperforming B. If you plot these values on successive days or weeks or months you get a line graph that is either sloping up or down or is horizontal. If the line slopes up A is outperforming B, and if it slopes down A is underperforming B, while if it is horizontal A is equally performing B. I prefer to use a daily chart for this. If you now add a 35 day sma to the chart it makes it easier to visualize outperformance and underperformance to the market. If you add a daily PPO(12,26,9) above, this shows you the momentum of the relative strength. With the daily chart for relative strength not only must the relative strength line above the 35 day ema, but the 35 day ema should be sloping up to confirm the trade is outperforming the market.

When you look at the price chart of an etf, industry or stock you can see if its sloping up, down or is moving horizontally, but you cant tell if its outperforming SPY (the market). To determine if its outperforming the market you need to put it into a daily relative strength chart eg. MSFT:SPY with a 35 day simple moving average, and also add a daily "relative PPO"(the PPO of MSFT:SPY) to show the momentum of the relative strength. When the relative strength line is above the 35 day sma and has been above it for at least a month, and both are sloping upward, and the relative PPO line is sloping up, above 0, and ideally above 1.0, you have a trade that is outperforming the market and has some sustainability. So when I am evaluating ETFs and industries I look at their relative strength charts. In my chartlist's I have a chartlist for Relative Strength of Industries and Relative Strength of ETF Sectors and etf Subsectors, so I can bring up a relative strength chart for these entities quickly. I also include relative strength in most of my chartstyles

     You can also get an idea of relative strength by running the scan [daily pctrelative(22,SPY)]. This scan shows you the outperformance or underperformance over 1 month of the trade to SPY. You can change the timespan if you wish to a day, a week, 6 mo or a year. You can also rankcharts in a chartlist using Rank by [daily pctrelative(22,spy)].

     To make the selection process of stocks and etfs more rapid and efficient I run my scans for top etf Sectors, top etf Subsectors, to Industries and top Stocks, and rank the trades generated by [daily pctrelative(22,SPY). I then bring up the candidates in my daily Keltner Channel chartstyle, study the chart, and see if the candidate is outperforming the market, its industry and the industry is also outperforming the market. I will then check the daily candlestick chartstyle for the trade and study the candlestick patterns and its relation to the emas, Keltner channel and Ichimoku cloud.

     From the above process I select the top etfs, industries, and stocks that are outperforming the "market" (SPY). I run thru the above process at least once a month and place the candidates in their respective top Sectors, top Subsectors, Top Industries and top Stocks chartlists.

     One has to get a general idea of what is going on inthe "Market". To accomplish this I first look at my chartlist for "Asset Classes" This divides the entire market universe into 5 asset classes:

     US stocks-SPY

     Foreign stocks -VEU

     Bonds-BND

Commodities-GSG

gold--GLD

I then rank the asset classes by weekly ROC(25)- 6mo. This shows you which asset classes are leading or lagging and gives you a general idea of what is going on in the market. If Bonds are leading this signifies that the market is bearish. If stocks are leading it indicates the market is bullish etc. So this gives you andidea of where you should be directing your interest.

To select the top stocks to trade I run my scans for top stocks.This usually generates around 50 to 100 candidates, and ranks them by ROC(12) - 3mo return.. I now place this list in "Summary" form with a 3 month time period.This shows the industry the candidates are in, their SCTR, and their 3 month pct-change. I prefer to choose stocks to trade that are in the top Industry list. I only look for stocks that are in the SP500, SP400, SP600, DOW30, or NASDAQ100 indexes. To be in these indexes the stock must have passed certain criteria determined by the index makers. I also require that the stock have a market cap of 6,500 or greater(this means six billion five hundred thousand), a price of $7.50 or greater, a daily trading volume of 400,000 or greater, and a SCTR >= 60. I then check the previous quarters earnings and sales report on Zacks. To be a candidate it must have beaten both earnings and sales estimates (a requirement recommended by Tom Bowley). On my daily Keltner channel chart the stock must be outperforming the "market", the stock must be outperforming its industry, and the industry must be outperforming the "market". I will also run a top stock scan for stocks with market cap between 6,500 and 350, however most of my choices are with stocks whose market cap is greater than 6,500. I also require the Keller ranking system to show the trade being in an uptrend long term intermediate term and short term.

I dont rely on Analysts ratings of a stock. Lots of stocks with bearish analyst ratings will have great charts, great relative strength, are in top industries and have beaten both earnings and revenues in their last quarterly earnings report. I rely on the chart and the price action. If the stocks price is rising, if the daily chart looks great, if the technical indicators I use look good, and the stock is in a strong industry, and the stock beats both earnings and revenues in its last earnings report, then I consider it a candidate and am not concerned about its other fundamentals or what analysts are saying about it. If you feel you need to consult an analyst rating to help choose between stocks then then Stochcharts offers a rating system, the Chaikin Power gauge on its dashboard, but I have found that stocks with any rating above bearish can be candidates using this system. Fidelity also offers a free Starmine Analyst rating on any stock.

I do the initial selection of stocks at the beginning of each new quarter(see below) and I try to hold these stocks thru an entire quarter. I would recommend investing anywhere from $200 to $2,500 in each trade depending on what you can afford. If the trade start doing well and increases in value by 5% over a couple of weeks I double the original investment. If the trade now increases to 7.5% I triple the original investment. If it then increases to a 10% gain I quadruple the original investment. I prefer this gradual increase in the commitment to a trade rather than placing $10,000 in a trade all at once, because it allows you to see how the trade is behaving, and if it is worthwhile to increase the amount of funds commited to the trade. Not infrequently you choose a good stock or etf and it either starts dropping in value or goes nowhere, while your other choices are trading higher and higher. I follow around 60 active stock trades and 15 ETF trades over the quarter in my trading account (see below). It is best to choose most of the top stocks to trade from the current top industry list. I refresh the current top etf, top industry, and top stock chartlist at the beginning of each month, and I will concentrate most of my stock selections in the top five industries. I will however occasionally select a stock to trade from an industry that is not outperforming the market if the stock shows very strong outperformance to the "market' and relative strength on the chart.

You have to be careful about overtrading stocks in the trading account, and etfs in the investment account. Your goal is to select top stocks in top industries and top etfs, and hold them thru the entire quarter, and thru their earnings report. If the stock had a negative earnings report and failed to beat estimated earnings and sales, then sell it and replace it with a new top stock in a top industry. If it beat earnings and sales estimates but issued a negative "guidance" report on future sales and earnings sell it. If it beat earnings and sales estimates but for some reason gapped down then watch if for a week. If it beat earnings and sales estimates and gaps up hold onto it.

If your trade starts to pullback or move horizontally this is normal. Any trade that was in a strong uptrend with a good price rise can pullback or enter a horizontal consolidation.. This is because some traders will sell the trade to collect profits, the trade could be "overbought" and buying pressure diminishes, manipulation by marketmakers is occuring to drive down the price so they can purchase it cheaper, it takes the market some time to digest the recent gains in price and uptrend. If the trade was in a good uptrend and starts moving horizontally or pulls back to the 25 day ema, or even the 50 day sma, and the slope of the 50,105 and 200 day moving averages is up, the slope of the Keltner Channel is up,the slope of Ichimoku cloud is up, the close if above the daily upper Keltner Channel(105,3.0,30), and the the daily sma(2, RSI(14)) is at or above 50, you can stay in the trade.

You must also remember and use the definition of an uptrend and down trend. An up trend is a series of higher highs and higher lows on the daily chart. A downtrend is a series of lower highs and lower lows on the daily chart. If you are in a trade and it develops a lower high and lower low after a good move up you have a trend change.

If your stock trade has an unexpected drop in value this can be due to a poor earnings report, an analysts downgrade,or some sudden macroeconomic change. To see what happened enter in your search engine box on your web browser "why did stock MU fall in price today" and the answer will appear. The same search method can also be used to understand why a stock has a sudden unexpected rise in value. If your trades appear on the exit scan, then its usually wise to exit them.

Further notes on trading:

1. if the "market regime" is bearish I dont enter any new trades in stocks or etfs, dont enter any new quarterly trades, sell any current stock or etf trades, and practice "capital preservation"(see chapter on hedging a portfolio).

2. If the market regime is bullish but the permission to trade long scan becomes negative I will hold off entering any new trades until the permisssion to trade long scan becomes positive again.

3. If the weekly close for SPY crosses below its 21 week ema(105 day ema), I will sell all my current stock and etf trades and up to 25% of my stake in SPY(see chapter on hedging).

4. If the market regime is bullish you can follow trades longer and ride thru any pullbacks that dont exceed the 50 day sma, especially if the permission to trade long scan remains positive.

5. Trades that have strong gains eg. 18% or more since you bought the trade at the beginning of the quarter.

Just because a trade has strong developed strong gains that doesnt mean that it will maintain them thru the quarter. The trade could loose half or all of its gains, or even turn into a loosing trade as the quarter progresses. To guard against this possibility i monitor all my stock and etf trades daily by placing all my stock trades in the "current intermediate trade" chartlist, and all my etf trades in the "current investment account" chartlist in the charstlye "chart for exiting current stock and etf trades". If a trade develops strong gains I change the color of the 50 day ema from purple to red, and I move the 50 day ema up or down in value to achieve a "best fit moving average" to the lows of the 2 day sma over the past month or two. If the sma(2,daily close) then crosses to or below the "best fit moving average +5, I exit the strong gain trade to preserve most of my gains. I place this chart in my recent trades chartlist and watch it. If the trade shows a "reversal" and starts moving up again I will reenter he trade with the original amount of cash that I first purchased it with.

6. Topping Patterns:

when a trade starts to top out and reverse after a strong rise usually the momentum indicators (PPO and RSI) start deteriorating, the candlestick bodies start shrinking in size and begin to move horizontally, Doji,inverted hammers, bullish engulfing, three black crows and other bearish reversal candlestick patterns can form, and reversal patterns like head and shoulder tops or double tops can form.

7. Momentum is another indicator that should be included in determining which trade to purchase. The significance of momentum is that it tends to persist over short periods of time(3 to 6 months). In other words if a stock shows good

momentum it is more likely to show good momentum over the next 3 to 6 months.

Momentum is measured by ROC(rate of change in price over a period of time). ROC = change in price over given period/ daily close in price or sma(50,daily close). So to measure momentum I use [weekly ROC(25)-6 mo, or weekly ROC(12) -3 mo. To incorporate momentum into a scan I scan for stocks with weekly ROC(25) >= 10, weeklyROC(12) >= 5,Weekly ROC(4) >= 1.66, and weekly ROC(1) > 0. This also incorporates realtive strength as the required percentage change are double those of the average returns for SPY over the same period.

8. Remaining in a trade for Stocks:

if 1. the market regime is bullish

2. if the permission to trade long scan is positiv

3. the sma(2,daily close) > sma(50,daily close)

4. if the sma(2,daily close) is above the daily upper Keltner Channel(105,3.0,30)

5. if the moving averages are in the proper order (25 day ema above 50 day sma,50 day sma above the 105 day ema, and 105 day ema above the 200 day ema), and they are sloping up

6. if the Keltner Channel and the *Ichimoku Cloud are sloping up*

7. *if the RSI(14) >= 40*

then you can remain in this trade as long as you wish and any fluctuations in the closing price that remain above the sma(50,daily close) could be considered "Noise"!!! This is an important concept to remember and will prevent you from overtrading.

.

" Short Term Trading"(days to a month):

When I started trading I would engage in some short term trading, however as I became more serious about investing and trading I found that all I could handle with the time I had available was intermediate term trading in my investment accounts and my trading portfolio. I simply didn't have the time to engage in short term trading even after I retired. Just to run my investment accounts (IRAs and non-IRA investment accounts) and my intermediate term trading account, and my readings in finance took all the time I set aside for investing and trading. I just dont have the time to do both, and managing my investments and trading intermediate term is more important to me. However I will include a short discourse on short term trading(days to weeks to a month) below and describe what I learned about it.

Trading Pullbacks:

This is a whole different category from investing. Here you are interested in finding short term trades that were in a strong uptrend an have pulled back, where you enter on the reversal of the pull back and remain in the trade for 4 or 5 days, or if the trade exceeds the previous high and looks strong you could stay in the trade for the length of the rally. You find these trades with scans for pullbacks(see the details of the pullback scans in the chapter on scans). What you are looking for here are stocks that were in a strong uptrend and then enter a "pullback" with a drop in price of at least 4% or greater. Ideally the stocks would be in strong industries and the industries would be in strong sectors, and the pullback would not exceed the daily sma(50) moving average. The 50,105 and 200 day moving averages should be sloping up, as should the Ichimoku cloud and the daily Keltner Channel. The SCTR value before the pull back should have been at least 75, and the [daily sma(2, RSI(14))] value should have been at least 60 before the pullback. The pullback scans should be run daily and the stocks generated should be placed in the "pullback chartlist". This can be done automatically in Stockcharts.com by using the "Scheduled Scan tool" in the "Members Tool" section.

To enter a pullback trade the trade must undergo a "reversal" from the pullback. This occurs when you get a candlestick with a higher high than the previous days high, and the previous days close is below the previous days ema(5,daily close). To enter the trade you must get a confirmation of this reversal, which is a candlestick with the close above the 5 day ema on the daily candlestick chart, with a higher high than the previous days high.

You stay in these trades a maximum of 4 days and usually sell on the close of the 4th day in the trade. You are looking for a gain of 3 to 4% or greater. If the trades close reaches or crosses above th peak in the sma(2,daily close) before the pullback you could stay in it until the "rally" was over as indicated by the close falling below th best fit moving average. I dont use a stop loss on these trades, but after I enter the trade if the close falls below the 5 day ema I exit the trade. To evaluate these trades I use my my candlestick chart with a 4 mo. time span, and I have a scan for "pullback stocks with a reversal" and this is also run as a scheduled scan every day on the pullback chartlist. The stocks it generates are placed in the "pullback with a reversal chartlist". Depending on what you can afford I would recommend entering these trades with anywhere from $200 to $3,000.

If you are trading short term not only should the market regime be bullish but you also dont want to be fighting short term downward trends in the market. You dont want SPY to be entering a pullback, or developing falling price momentum. I have therefore developed a "permission to trade long" scan which insures that the short term trend of the market is strong. If the permission to trade long scan is negative I hold off doing any short term trades until it turns positive.

Trading Gaps, True Breakouts and new 3 mo, 6 mo, or 12 mo New Highs):

Gaps up are usually due to strong earnings reports but can also follow an analyst upgrade, or a stock being acquired by another company. A significant number of gaps up are followed by pullbacks that attempt to close the gap partially or fully. Therefore I dont enter gap trades on the gap up. I wait for a pullback and enter on the reversal, and either exit the trade at the end of the rally from the pullback, or keep the trade and add it to my quarterly stock trades.

True Breakouts are trades where the daily high exceeds the max daily high over the year starting one month ago, and the daily highs in the current month except for day 1 are less than the max daily high over the year starting 1 month ago. In other words you get a breakout from a base, not a steady climb up where each day represent a new high. They also behave like gaps up and tend to develop pullbacks during the first couple of weeks, however these pullbacks tend to be less and of shorter duration than the pullbacks in gaps up. Therefore, I dont wait for the pull back to enter the trades. I do wait for "confirmation" to enter these trades. Confirmation means that on the day after the breakout from a base the high is higher than the high on the day of the breakout. I hold these trades through a rally and exit with the cross of price below the best fit moving average, or if they are in top industries they can be kept and added to your quarterly stock trades.

New 3 mo or 12 mo Highs are trades in an uptrend that reach new highs over the specified time period. They dont breakout from a base and tend to form consecutive new highs every day. New Highs indicate strong uptrends, and trades that show this characteristic can be considered for trading in you intermediate term trades. A trade that reaches a new 3 or 12 mo high are exceptionally strong and should seriously be considered for your trading account, and should be incorporated into your scheduled scans. I always run the new 3 and 12 mo scans in addition to my scan tor top stocks, top etfs, and top industries.

Having a "Mentor":

I think its important for a novice to have a "mentor", a professional, knowledgeable investor and trader to review the market for them and teach them how to further their investing and trading skills. I would recommend Dave Keller who writes blogs for Stockcharts.com and has his own website(www.marketmisbehaviour.com). His daily blog "the final bar with Dave Keller" reviews the activity in the market each day after the close, and his additional blogs on Stockcharts.com are dedicated to teaching investors and traders about the market. He is a great "teacher". He also has a subscription service for those wanting further advice and recommendations. Tom Bowley at Stockcharts is also a good teacher and a sophisticated trader, and his articles are always worthwhile reading. Mary Ellen McGonicle at Stockcharts has a nice basic method of trading based on the Investors Daily Newspaper technique using th MACD, RSI(14) and the 50 day sma.

I would also recommend the Yahoo Finance Morning Brief. This is a free e-mail subscription that sends you an e-mail each morning summarizing the previous days important market developments and a summary of the days important economic developments. I also read the Wall Street Journal every day.

In Summary"

The market regime must be bullish and the permission to trade long scan should be positive to select etfs and stocks for the quarterly trades in investment and trading accounts, and to trade pullbacks. To select etfs and stocks for the investment and trading accounts they should appear on the scans for top etfs and stocks, and the stocks should predominantly be in the industries from the top industries scan chartlist. You enter these trades immediately at the "beginning"(see below) of a new quarter, and you try to hold them thru the entire quarter and thru their earnings report.

For pullback trades your enter on a "reversal" and hold the trade for 4 days and then sell automatically. However if they are in a top industry and the chart looks good you could hold them thru the entire "rally". For gaps up you wait for a pullback and then trade them as pull back trades. For breakouts you enter on the confirmation(the high is above the high on the breakout) and hold them thru the rally or longer. For New Highs you can enter immediately if the trade is in a top industry.

Remember:

A. 1. if the market regime is bullish

2. and the permission to trade long is positive

3. and the slope of the moving averages and the Kelt Chan and the Ichimoku cloud are up

4. and the sma(2,daily close) is above the 50 day sma, and above the upper Kelt Chan

5. and the daily moving averages are in the proper order with the 25 above the 50, and the 50 above the 105, and the 105 above the 200, and are sloping up

6. and the upper Kelt Chan is above the Ichimoku Cloud Top and both are sloping up

7. and the daily sma(2,RSI(14)) is above 40

Then any fluctuations of the sma(2,daily close) in stocks that remain above the 50 day ema can be considered "Noise," and you can remain in the trade!!!! I dont use stop losses on quarterly trades, I use the above and my exit criteria.

B. if the market regime becomes bearish, or the sma(2,daily close) for SPY crosses below the daily sma(105,daily close) You exit all trades.

The above represents a distillation of what I have found useful and important. It presents a basic method of dealing with the "market", investing and managing your investments. There are many other more sophisticated methods that incorporate data science, computer algorithms, options, macroeconomics,

proprietary indicators and scans, etc. that professional traders and hedge funds utilize. There are many more aggressive methods of dealing with the "market" incorporating trading options, futures and currencies. What I have presented here is a method that a non-professional, novice investor and trader could use to function in the market and keep out of trouble. After you have been investing and trading for a couple of years using the above "safety curtain" then you may be ready to branch out on your own and expand and explore different investing and trading venues. It appears to me that achieving success in investing and trading in addition to identifying the market regime revolves around two things, the trade selection process and the trade exiting process, and they are both equally important. Over the past few year's I think that market volatility has increased. If you take your chart list of ETF Sectors and rank them every week by [daily pctrelative(22,SPY) you will see the rapidity with which sector rotation occurs. To achieve success, you must be vigilant and keep abreast of these changes.

I was interested in learning how to invest and trade so that I could run my own investments intelligently, make a little money trading, not have to devote all day to doing this, and try to be successful in this challenge. I prefer to manage my own affairs if possible and not relegate them to another party. I consider managing ones finances a basic "survival skill" that everyone needs know something about. If I had the information presented in this book when I started investing and trading 50 years ago, I would be wealthier than I am today, and I would have avoided most of the mistakes I made in the investing and trading learning curve.

There are other benefits to actively managing an investment and trading account, especially when you are retired.

1. It gives you something interesting, challenging and time consuming to do in retirement.

2. It keeps your mind active and makes you think.

3. It keeps you engaged in what is going on in the world.

4. It teaches you discipline, organization, and risk management.

5. you can make some money in retirement without having to leave your home..

The purpose of this book is to teach a novice how to invest and trade. There are whole areas of knowledge related to investing and trading that I have not discussed like Inflation, Money Supply, the Fed and Economics. These constitute a vast area of knowledge that I would recommend every investor and trader try to educate themselves in. These are all interrelated, and complicated subject matters that can have a direct bearing on the "market". It is a huge body of information and study material. It is important to have some basic understanding of these subjects.

Chapter 5.   ETFs and Mutual Funds

ETFs and mutual funds have similarities and differences. They both consist of groups of stocks or bonds that can represent an index, a sector, an industry, a style (eg. Growth, value ,capitalization size, etc.), active management, passive management, etc. They differ in that ETFs can be traded throughout the day at the current market price, whereas mutual funds can only be bought and sold at the close of the market for the closing price. On charts there is a significant difference in that mutual funds are represent by a line chart whose value changes on the close of the market, whereas ETFs appear on charts as stocks do with an open, close, high and low. ETFs can be traded freely and be sold anytime(within a day week, month etc. after purchase), while mutual funds have time restrictions on trading an usually have to be held for a month or longer to avoid trading penalties. The managing fees of mutual funds are in general much higher than that of ETFs. If you hold ETFs in a non-IRA account they don't throw off any or very little capital gains distributions on which you would have to pay taxes, whereas mutual funds can generate significant amounts of capital gains. For some of the above reasons I prefer to invest and trade in ETFs rather than mutual funds with one exception, the Fidelity Select Sector mutual funds(see below).

I consider all high dividend yielding investments to be in the "bond" category like dividend ETFs, preferred Stock ETFs, convertible security ETFs, covered call ETFs, as well as conventional bond ETFs. In my investment portfolios they are all part of the bond portfolio. I never trade or sell the "bond" portion of my investment portfolios, even in a bearish market regime, because doing so would interrupt the compounding effect on the growth of the portfolio which is just or even more important, and more stable than the price appreciation of individual ETF.

ETFs:

This is a list of the ETFs that I have found useful and will invest in and trade, in addition to SPY when the market regime is bullish, and the permission to trade long scan is positive, and the ETF is outperforming the market(SPY). They all have decent market cap and daily trading volume.

1. Etfs for my investment accounts:

I will trade any of the Sector etfs-XLK,XLC,XLY,XLB,XLI,XLF,XLRE,XLP and XLU-that are outperforming the market in ny investment account. I give preference to the sector etfs over the subsector etfs. In the subsector etfs the next group I give preference too are growth vs value etfs like SPYG,IUSG,SMH,QQQ,FBCG,SPMO,SPYV,IUSV,VTV. This is followed by the market cap group like MGC,OEF,IWM,MDY and IWC. Finally I look for etfs in the SubSectors groups that are outperforming the market like Commodity etfs, large cap blend etfs, subsectors in technology, healthcare, consumer discretionary, artifical intelligence, financials, realestate, home construction, renewable energy, transportation, mining, and precious metals.

I also hold the following large cap blend etfs permanently in my investment accounts and dont trade them. These include:

FDL,FNDX,PKW,SPHD,SPHQ,SPLV, USMV,MOAT,VIG,VV, RSP,RWL,QUAL,SCHD,SCHX,RSP,NOBL,ESGU,COWZ.

I will also trade the Fidelity Select Portfolio Mutual Funds. These represent the selections of the younger , smart, analysts at Fidelity in the various sectors, and are frequently the top choice in a sector or industry. You must hold these trades at least a full month or Fidelity will stop you from trading them, thus they differ from ETFs which can be bought and sold without restrictions. So. if you enter a trade in one of these and it starts to deteriorate before a month is up you can't exit it until the end of the monthly holding period.

FBIOX, FBMPX, FBSOX, FCYIX, FDCPX, FDFAX, FDLSX, FIDSX, FNARX, FPHAX, FSAGX, FSAVX, FSCHX, FSCPX, FSCPX ,FSCSX, FSDAX, FSDPX, FSELX, FSENX, FSHOX, FSLBX ,FSLEX, FSMEX, FSPCX, FSHX, FSPTX, FSRBX, FSSRFX, FSRPX, FSTCX, FSUTX, FSVLX, FWRLX

I try to hold the new quarterly etfs for the entire trading quarter, but if their Daily RSI(14) falls below 40 and their daily sma(2,daily close) drops below the daily sma(50,daily close) I will sell them. I also monitor their relative strength to SPY ($SYMBOL:SPY) and if the daily sma(2,$Symbol:SPY) crossses below the daily sma(35,$Symbol:SPY) I would be inclined to sell the trade.

The "Bond" ETFs I trade:

See above section on Investing.

Ex-Dividend date Considerations in selling ETFs in the IRA and non-IRA investment accounts:

To receive a dividend in the above ETFs you must own it 1 day prior to the ex-dividend date, so if you wish to sell an ETF in which you have a substantial position, and the ex-dividend date is close at hand it may be worthwhile to wait and sell it one day after the ex-dividend date. To determine the ex- dividend date you go to Fidelity-Research-ETFs-distributions and expenses.

To find the composition(the stocks in an etf) of an etf use www.Fundvidualizer.com or Fidelity-Research=ETFs.

Chapter 6.   The Quarterly Method of Trading

The quarters are 3 month periods beginning in January,April,July, and October. "Earnings Season" when most publicly traded companies report their quarterly earnings and revenues starts around the 3rd Monday in the first month of a quarter, and ends around the 3rd Friday in the 2nd month of the quarter. To see the exact dates check the free Zacks earnings calendar. The majority of significant stock earnings reports occur during this interval.

The 3rd Friday of the 3rd month in a quarter is when monthly stock options, monthly stock indexes options and monthly futures options expire simultaneously. This is known as "triple witching" This result is increased market volatility during that week and the Monday and Tuesday of the following week. Part of the increased volatility is due to "market makers" manipulating the market by selling short stocks that are optionable and have significantly increased in price of the past month, or buying stocks that have fallen in price significantly over the past month. They also do the same with indexes such as $SPX, and QQQ.

Market Makers(large financial firms) are prime sellers of puts and calls, and if there is a large imbalance in the number of calls over puts in a stock or index that has risen in price over the past month, or if the is a large imbalance in the number of puts overcalls in stocks or indexes that have fallen then to reduce financial losses the market makers will sell short stocks that have risen to reduce their "strike" price and render the calls at those strikes worthless, or buy stocks that have fallen to increase their "strike" price and render the puts at those strikes worthless. This manipulation can start on Wednesday before the Friday options expiration and last into the next week and is over by the close on the following Tuesday.

To avoid watching your optionable stocks with good gains fall in price during this period one has to use the above information to counteract the market makers. Thus I now sell all my quarterly trades on the the close Tuesday the week of "triple witching"(the 3rd Friday in the 3rd month of a quarter. I can now either purchase my new quarterly trades on the open Wednsday following triple witching, or hold off repurchasing even longer depending on market conditions, but not beyond the end of the monthly quarter. Waiting until after triple witching or the actual end of the quarter allows one to evaluate new trades and see where the Sector Rotation of the ETF sectors and industries is heading to make a decision on which sectors and industries you wish to be in for the new quarter.

I will try to hold these quarterly trades thru their earnings report and sell on the close Tuesday the week of triple witching. However , if a trade starts to deteriorate and develops the exit criteria described above I will sell before its earnings report and replace it with a new trade.

Trading using the above quarterly method also has other advantages.

1. It allows you to capture your gains and losses in a timely fashion.The longer you hold a position in a trade the riskier the trade becomes,as most trades will "mean revert"(fall back to their mean price (eg the 25 day ema) over time. Thus it reduces your risk.

2. It allows you to deal with the market rotations that are continuously occuring (eg. growth vs value, large cap vs small cap, risk on(aggressive stocks and sectors) vs risk off(defensive stocks and sectors)

3.. It allows you to wait until the end of the quarter to deliberate and see where things are heading.

4. It gives you the opportunity to change your mind on a trade you thought had promise but isn't doing well.

Chapter 7.   Hedging IRA and non-IRA investment portfolios in a bearish market regime("Capital Preservation"):

Definitions:

1. Pullback in SPY(the market) is where the close is less than 10% below a recent max high.

2. A Correction in SPY(the market) is where the close has dropped between 10% and less than 20% from a recent max high.

3. A Bear Market in SPY is where the close has dropped 20% or more from a recent max high in SPY or the weekly close has crossed below the lower Kelt Chan(21,1.50,20) or the 40 week sma(200 day sma on the daily chart), whichever comes first.

In my investment portfolios I have 50% of the stock etf portion in SPY and the other 50% in other "blend" type etfs. Hedging a portfolio   involves selling 100% of your holding in the SPY etf portion when the market regime turns bearish, placing that money in cash, and reinvesting back in SPY when the market "bottoms".

To "Hedge" a portfolio:

1.when the close of SPY falls below the 105 day ema or below the 21 week ema you sell all your trades in outperforming ETFS in the investment accounts, and all the stocks in you trading account, and place the money in cash. You now sell enough of SPY to equal 25% of your Stake in SPY(stake in SPY = amt in SPY plus amt of cash from selling outperforming etfs in the investment accounts.)

2. If the close of SPY now falls below the 30 week ema(150 day ema) you sell another 25% of your stake in SPY and place the money in cash.

3. If the close of SPY now falls below the 200 day sma, or below the lower weekly Keltner Channel(21,1.50,20), or below the lower daily Keltner Channel(105,3.0,30)(whichever comes first), you sell the remaining 50% of your stake in SPY and place the money in cash.

4. When the market bottoms you reinvest all the cash in SPY. You stay in SPY until the "market regime" becomes bullish (weekly close of SPY crosses above the weekly upper Keltner Chanel(21,1.50,20), and the weekly upper Kelt Chan is above the weekly Ichimoku Cloud Top). At that point you can start trading stocks and etfs that are outperforming the market again.

note. The above with reguards to SPY only hold for the IRAs. In the non-IRA investment accounts(if you have them) you only sell your ETF trades in the investment accounts and your stock trades in the trading account and place that money in cash and reinvest it in SPY at the market bottom. You dont sell SPY because hedging a non IRA portfolio is not indicated due to the capital gains and associated taxes it could generate.

The following is an analysis of the financial outcome of this simple hedging technique:

A. IRA investment Portfolio- No Hedging done in a bearish market regime:

$1,000,000 stock etf IRA portfolio with 12.5% in stock etfs outperforming the market, 37.5%% in SPY, and 50% in other blend ETFs, and with $200,000 in long term capital gains; market regime becomes bearish and market drops 25%; no hedging done.

At market bottom portfolios is now worth $750,000

Drawdown is 25%

Market rises 30% in next 6-8 mo. and you end up with

(750,000 + 750,000 x 0.30) = 750,000 + 225,000 = $975,000

B. IRA investment portfolio as above with hedging:

SPY drops 6% and has crossed below the 21. wk ema(105 day ema), and you now sell all the etfs you hold that are outperforming the market and enough SPY to account for 25% of your stake in SPY(12.5% of your total stock stake.You now have ($1,000,000-0.06 x $1,000,000) left which equals $940,000 with $150,000 in cap gains, and 12.5% of it is now in cash(940,000 x 0.125) = $117,500 in cash and $822,500 still in stock etfs.You dont have to worry about any taxes on capital gains involved in selling some of the etfs because capital gains in an IRA are not taxed.

The market now declines another 4% and crosses below the 150 day ema or 30 week ema. So you are left with (822,500 - 0.04 x 822,500) = $789,600 in stock etfs of which 37.5% is SPY. You now sell another 12.5% of your stake in SPY = $789,600 x 0.125 = $98,700 in SPY to achieve a 50 % sale in SPY. You are now left with (789,600 - 98,700) = $690,900 in stock etfs and (117,500 + 98,700) = $216, 200 in cash.

The market now drops another 4% for a total of 14% and the close crosses below the weekly lower Keltner Channel(21,1.50,20) or below the daily lower Keltner Channel(105,3.0,30)]. You are now left with with(690,900-0.04 x 690,900) = $663,264 in stock etfs of which 25% is in SPY. You now sell the remainder of SPY(25% of the $663,264) and you are left with(663,264 - 0.25 x663,264) =$496,448 in non SPY stock etfs, and $165,816 in cash +$216,200 cash from above = total of $496,448 in stock etfs and $382,016 in cash.

The market now drops another 11% to give a total drop of 25% and you are left with $382,016 in cash and (496,448 - 0.11x 496,448) = $441,839 in non SPY stock etfs at the market bottom for a total of $823,855.

Your "Drawdown" is now $1,000,000 - $823,855 = $176,145/$1,000,000 = 17.61% instead of 25% with no hedging.

Over the next 6 to 8 months the market rises 30% and you end up with a total of (823,855 + 823,265 x 0.30) = $1,071,011 in stock etfs which is $96,011 more than if you did no hedging(capital preservation).

In summary you sell 25% of your stake in SPY when the market(SPY) drops below the 21 week ema(105 day ema), and another 25%of your stake in SPY when the market (SPY) drops below the 30 wk ema(150 day ema), and the final 50% of your stake in SPY) when the market(SPY) drops below the lower weekly Kelt Chan(21,1.50,20), or below the 200 day sma on the daily chart(whichever comes first).. You reinvest all the cash back into SPY at the market bottom(see chapter on market bottoms).(note: you dont have to worry about the " wash rule" here as it doesnt apply to IRAs.

The above is basically an "algorithmic" method of gradually exiting 50% of your entire stock portfolio in a potential bearish market regime. It allows you to make definitive decisions without waivering when the market conditions become negative.

I dont feel comfortable selling the entire stock portfolio and being totally out of the market. I think selling 50% of it is a reasonable compromise.

There are many other sophisticated methods of hedging a portfolio in a potential bear market such as using options, inverse SPY etfs, and Gold, but I dont have any experience with these and I think for novices the above method is doable.

C. Non-IRA investment portfolio with hedging:

I have done the calculations for a non-IRA investment portfolio with hedging and you end up around 10 to 15% less in total portfolio value after the 30% rise from a market bottom. So (1,075,444 - 0.125 x 1,075,444 = $941,013 which is less than if you did no hedging at all. Thus in my opinion it is not worth to try and hedge a non-IRA investment portfolio with significant capital gains because of the federal taxes it generates, other than selling your ETFs outperforming the market in your non-IRA investment account and the stocks in your trading account. You dont sell SPY!

Chapter 8   Industry Relative Strength to SPY Chartlist:

This is a daily chart of 1.5yrs duration with the Symbol being the Symbol for the industry: SPY, eg. $DJUSRA:SPY, and a daily sma(35) moving average. It also has a daily PPO line(12,26,9) above of the $SYMBOL:$SPX. To be a strong industry the relative strength line must be above the sma(35) line for at least a month, both the relative strength line and the 35 day sma should be sloping up, and the relative PPO line(momentum of the relative strength) must be above 0 . I look at both the weekly relative strength charts and the daily relative strength charts.

$DJUSAS:SPY Aerospace index

$DJUSAR:SPY Airlines Index

$DJUSAL:SPY Aluminum index

$DJUSRA:SPY Apparel Retailers Index

$DJUSAG:SPY Asset Managers Index

$DJUSAT:SPY Auto Parts Index

$DJUSAU:SPY Automobile Index

$DJUSBK:SPY Banks Index

$DJUSBT:SPY Biotechnology Index

$DJUSDB:SPY Brewers Index

$DJUSBC:SPY Broadcasting & Entertainment Index

$DJUSRB:SPY Broadline Retailers Index

$DJUSBD:SPY Building Materials & Fixtures Index

$DJUSIV:SPY Business Support Services Index

$DJUSBE:SPY Business Training & Employment Agencies

$DJUSCF:SPY Clothing & Accessories Index

$DWCCOA:SPY Coal Index

$DJUSHR:SPY Commercial Vehicles & Trucks Index

SDJUSCC:SPY Commodity Chemicals Index

$DJUSCR:SPY Computer Hardware Index

$DJUSDV:SPY Computer Services Index

$DJUSSF:SPY Consumer Finance Index

$DJUSCP:SPY Containers & Packaging Index

$DJUSVE:SPY Conventional Electricity Index

$DJUSDN:SPY Defense Index

$DJUSAF:SPY Delivery Services Index

$DJUSVN:SPY Distillers & Vintners Index

$DJUSDT:SPY Diversified Riets

$DJUSRD:SPY Drug Retailers Index

$DJUSHD:SPY Durable Household Products Index

$DJUSEC:SPY Electrical Components & Equipment Index

$DJUSAI:SPY Electronic Equipment index

$DJUSOS:SPY Exploration & Production Index

$DJUSFA:SPY Financial Administration Index

$DJUSFC:SPY Fixed Line Telecommunications Index

$DJUSFP:SPY Food Products Index

$DJUSFD:SPY Food Retailers & Wholesalers Index

$DJUSFT:SPY Footwear Index

$DJUSIF:SPY Full Line Insurance Index

$DJUSFH:SPY Furnishings Index

$DJUSCA:SPY Gambling Index

$DJUSGU:SPY Gas Distribution Index

$DJUSMG:SPY General Mining Index

$DJUSPM:SPY Gold Mining Index

$DJUSHP:SPY Health Care Providers Index

$DJUSHV:SPY Heavy Construction Index

$DJUSHB:SPY Home Construction Index

$DJUSHI:SPY Home Improvement Retailers Index

$DJUSHL:SPY Hotel & Lodging REITS Index

$DJUSLG:SPY Hotels Index

$DJUSIO:SPY Industrial & Office REITS

$DJUSFE:SPY Industrial Machinery index

$DJUSDS:SPY Industrial Suppliers Index

$DJUSIB:SPY Insurance Brokers Index

$DJUSOL:SPY Integrated Oil & Gas Index

$DJUSNS:SPY Internet Index

$DJUSSB:SPY Investment Services

$DJUSIL:SPY Life Insurance Index

$DJUSAV:SPY Media Agencies Index

$DJUSMS:SPY Medical Supplies Index

$DJUSAM:SPY Medical Equipment Index

$DJUSMG:SPY Mining Index

$DJUSWC:SPY Mobile Telecommunications Index

$DJUSMF:SPY Mortgage Finance Index

$DJUSMR:SPY Mortgage REITS Index

$DJUSMU:SPY Multiutilities Index

$DJUSHN:SPY Nondurable Household Products Index

$DJUSNF:SPY Nonferrous Metals Index

$DJUSOI:SPY Oil Equipment & Services Index

$DWCPAP:SPY Paper Total Stock Market Index

$DJUSCM:SPY Personal Products Index

$DJUSPR:SPY Pharmaceuticals Index

$DJUSPL:SPY Pipelines Index

$DJUSIP:SPY Property & Casualty Insurance Index

$DJUSPB:SPY Publishing Index

$DJUSRR:SPY Railroad Index

$DJUSEH:SPY Real Estate Holding & Development Index

$DJUSES:SPY Real Estate Services

$DJUSRP:SPY Recreational Products Index

$DJUSRQ:SPY Recreational Services Index

$DJUSIU:SPY Reinsurance

$DWCREE:SPY Renewable Energy Equipment Index

$DJUSRN:SPY Residential REITS Index

$DJUSRU:SPY Restaurants & Bars Index

$DJUSGT:SPY Retailers Index

$DJUSSC:SPY Semiconductor Index

$DJUSSD:SPY Soft Drinks Index

$DJUSSW:SPY Software Index

$DJUSCS:SPY Specialized Consumer Services Index

$DJUSCX:SPY Specialty Chemicals Index

$DJUSSP:SPY Specialty Finance Index

$DJUSSR:SPY Specialty REITS

$DJUSRS:SPY Specialty Retailers Index

$DJUSST;SPY Steel Index

$DJUSCT:SPY Telecommunications Equipment Index

$DJUSTY:SPY Toys Index

$DJUSTS:SPY Transportation Services Index

$DJUSTT:SPY Travel &Tourism Index

$DJUSTK:SPY Trucking Index

$DJUSPC:SPY Waste & Disposal Services Index

$DJUSWU:SPY Water Index

Note: 1.To just get the pure Industry list you remove the :SPY from each of the above notations. The above list is the relative strength of the industries to SPY list.

2. by putting the industry relative strength chartlist in "Summary" form and choosing 1 wk, 1 mo, 3 mo, 6 mo, and YTD time frames you

get the relative strength percentage change which correlates well with the top industries for those time periods.

There are other ways to determine relative strength:

1. rank by [daily pctrelative(66,SPY)] = 3mo elative strength

rank by [daily pctrelative(126,SY)] = 6 mo relative strength, etc.

2.using the weekly $BPSECTOR (the percent of stocks in an Index or Sector) aabove 50%/

3. using the the weekly $SECTORHLP, the SECTOR new highs- new lows percent with chart type = Area

4.using the weekly ROC(25) or Weekly ROC(12) with chart type = performance. Here remember that for SPY the weekly ROC(25), the 6 mo ROC is 5%, and the weekly ROC(51), the 1 year ROC is 10% and you wantyour stock choices to be double the ROC for SPY.

Chapter 9.   My Chart styles parameters:

When you pull up a chart on Stockcharts.com on the left- hand side of the screen you see 12 small vertical rectangular boxes. This is where you name and store the chart-styles you wish to frequently use. To store a chart-style you first create the chart with the indicators and time span you wish to use and then go above the boxes and click the "arrow".This brings up the names of the chartstyles. You now click "edit" and on the bottom you will see "add new". You click on the empty box on the left and type in the name of your chartstyle and press done on the top.

Below is a list of the chart styles with their exact parameters that I have found useful.

1. weekly long term chart:

2 yr. time span, weekly chart

wkly. thick black line representing price

wkly. weekly ema(21:red), weekly sma(10:purple), weekly sma(40:brown)

wkly. Keltner Chan(21,1.50,20)-Area-Gray

weekly Ichimoku cloud

wkly. PPO line(12,26,9) above with horizontal line at 0 and 1.0

wkly RSI(14) above

wkly SCTR above with horizontal line at 75:black

wkly AccDist with sma(30) below

wkly Chaikin Money Flow(20) with horiz line at 0

wkly $SYMBOL:SPY with sma(30)

wkly $SYMBOL:$INDUSTRY with sma(30)

wkly $Industry: SPY with sma(30)

2. weekly 6mo. performance chart

   6mo time span with "type" performance in chart attributes

   solid red weekly price line

   horizontal dashed black lines at 10,5 and 1.66

3. daily Keltner Channel Chart

   1 yr. time span

   daily sma(2,daily close) black

   daily ema(25), sma(50), ema(105), and sma(200), and daily ema(5)-
   dashed thick line red

   daily Kelt Chan(105,3.0,30)

   daily Ichimoku Cloud

   daily PPO line(12,26,9) above

   daily sma(2,RSI(14)) above with horiz. lines at 40 and 60 above

   daily SCTR line above with horizontal lne at 75 above

   daily Chaikin Money Flow(20) below

   daily sma(2,Accum/Dist) below with sma(35) below

   daily sma(2,$SYMBOL:$SPX) with sma 35 below

   daily sma(2,$SYMBOL: $INDUSTRY) with sma 35 below

   daily sma(2,$INDUSTRY:$SPX) with sma 35 below

4. daily candlestick chart:

    1 yr time span

    Candlesticks

    daily ema(25),sma(50),ema(105), sma(200) and daily ema(5)-dashed thick red line

    daily Kelt Chan(105,3.0,30]

    daily Ichimoku cloud

    daily PPOline(12,26,9) above

    daily sma(2,RSI(14)) above with horiz. line at 40 and 60

    daily SCTR above with horizontal line at 75

    daily sma(2,AccDist) with ema(35) below

    daily CMF(20) below with horiz line at 0

    daily sma(2,ROC(50)) below with horiz line at 3.50 and 0

    daily sma(2,Slope(126)) below with horiz line at 0

5.   3 min. 2 day chart:

    2 day chart with 3 min. "Period"

    candlesticks

    volume behind price

6. Trend Indicator Chart(Mid to long term)(via D. Keller)_

    3year weekly chart

    price invisible

    weekly PPO line(21,34,0) behind price

    weekly PPO line(5,13,0) below

    weekly PPO line(1,5,0) below

7. Long Term Weekly Chart:

    weekly chrt with 6 yr time span

    weeky Candlestick price representation

    weekly Kelt Chan(21,1.50,20)

    weekly Ichimoku Cloud

8. Chart for exiting current stock and etf trades:

    daily chaart with 1 yr time span

    sma(2,daily close)

    sma(50,daily close) , ema(105,daily close) , sma(200,daily close)

    daily volume supeerimposed on price

    daily Kelt Chan(105,3.0,30)

    daiy Ichimoku cloud

    Daily RSI(14) above with horiz lines at 40,60,

    daily ROC(50) below with horiz. line at 3.50

daily sma(2,AccDist) below with sma(35)

daily Chaikin Money Flow (20) below

9. daily Relative Strength chart for stocks and etfs:

price invisible

$SYMBOL:SPY with sma(2,daily close) and sma(35,daily close) below

$SYMBOL:$INDUSTRY with sma(2) and sma(35) below

$INDUSTRY:SPY with sma(2) and sma(35) below

$SYMBOL:$SECTOR

10. Weekly Relative Strength Chart:

weekly chart with 5 yr time span

weekly sma(2,$SYMBOL:SPY) as thick line with sma(35)

weekly PPO(12,26,9,$SYMBOL:SPY)

Chapter 9.   My Chartlists

SPY (38)

ETF Sectors (#1)

ETF Subsectors (#191) and (#15)

Blend ETFs (#23)

Market Cap and Style ETFs (# 59) and (#186)

Fidelit Select Mutual Fuinds (#26))

Commodity ETFs (#47)

Industry list (#40)

Current Intermediate stock Trades(#223)

Current Investment Account ETF trades (#92)

Bonds I currently own #70

New 12 mo highs and 6 yr highs(41)

Chartlist 0 #34

Market Bottoms #20

Relative Strength of Industries to SPY #31

Relative Strength of ETF Sectors to SPY #21

Relative Strength of ETF SubSectors to SPY #204

Relative Strength of Commodities to SPY (93)

Gap up stocks   #207

To Watch-Stocks and ETFs #45

Top ETFs Sectors this month #177

Top ETF Sub Sectors this month 205

Top Industries this month #224

Top Stocks this month   #77

Top Commodities this month #61

top Fidelity Selects this month # 213

Chapter 10.   My Scans

One should copy these scans exactly into their list of scans and check the syntax after copying each scan. The criteria for these scans have been repeatedly checked to insure they provide good results. I consider these scans one of the most important part of the book.

1.0 Permission to Trade Long Scan:

[favorites list = 38] (this chartlist is $SPX)

and [daily ema(25,daily close) > daily sma(50,daily close)]

and daily ema(25,daily close) >= daily ema(105,daily close)]

and [daily ema(105,daily close) > daily sma(200,daily close)]

and [daily sma(2,daily close) > daily sma(50,daily close)]

and [daily sma(2,daily close) > daily upper Kelt Chan(105,3.0,30)]

and [daily upper Kelt Chan(105,3.0,30) > daily Ichimoku Cloud Top(9,26,52)]

and [daily PPO line(12,26,9,daily close) >= -0.25] aabove

and [daily RSI(14) >= 45] above

and [SCTR >= 50] above

and [daily sma(2,AccDist) >= daily sma(35, AccDist)] below

and [daily sma(2,Slope(20)) > 0] below

and [daily sma(2,ROC(15)) > 0] below

and [daily CMF(20) > 0] below

and [weekly close > weekly sma(10,weekly close)]

and [weekly upper Kelt Chan(21,1.50,20) > weekly

Ichimoku Cloud Top(9,26,52)]

and [weekly PPO line(12,26,9, weekly close) >= 0.50]

and [weekly RSI(14) >= 50]

1.10 Top Asset Class scan by 6 mo ROC:

favorites list = 242

and [weekly ppo line(1,5,0) > 0]

and [weekly ppo line(5,13,0) > 0]

and [weekly ppo line(21,34,0) > 0

and [weekly Slope(25) > 0]

(these a Kellers trend indicator criteria for short, intermediate and long term trend)

and [weeklyROC(25) >= 2]

and [weekly ROC(12) >= 1]

and [weekly ROC(4) >= 0.33]

and [weekly ROC(1) >= 0]

(these values are the same as for BND(Barclays US aggregate bond fund) with an 12 mo ROC of 4%, 6moROC of 2%, 3 mo ROC of 1% and weekly ROC > 0

and [daily ppo line(12,26,9,daily close) > 0]

and [daily RSI(14,daily close) >= 50]

and [SCTR >= 60]

and [daily close > daily sma(200,daily close)]

and [daily sma(2,daily close) > daily ema(25,daily close)]

and[daily sma(2,daily close) > daily upper Kelt Chan(105,3.0,30)] and [daily upper Kelt Chan(105,3.0,30) > daily Ichimmoku Cloud top(9,26,52)]

and [daily ema(25,daily close) > daily ema(105,daily close)]

and [daily ema(105,daily close) daily sma(200,daily close)]

Rank by [weeklyROC(25)

note: the above scan outline is repeated in all the following scans with the possible changes in the values of the weekly ROC.It incorporates momentum, relative strength, and chart architecture of an uptrend.

1.2 Top ETF Sector scan by 6mo(25 weeks) ROC:

[favorites list = 1]

all is the same as scan 1.10 except the values for the weekly ROC.Here use:

and [weekly ROC(25) >= 5]

and [weekly ROC(12) >= 2.50]

and Weekly ROC(4) >= 0.83]

and [weekly ROC(1) >= 0]

Rank by [weekly ROC(25)

1.3 Top ETF SubSector scan by 6 mo ROC:

    [[favorites list = 191] or [favorites list = 47]]

    all is the sma as scan 1.10 except the values for the weekly ROC. Here use:

        and [weekly ROC(25) >= 7.50]

        and [weekly ROC(12) >= 3.75]

        and [weekly ROC(4) >= 1.25]

        and [weeklyh ROC(1) >= 0]

1.4 Top ETF Blend scan by 6 mo ROC:

    [favorites list = 23]

    rest is same as scan 1.20 !!

1.5 Top ETF Cap and Style scan by 6 mo ROC:

    [favorites list = 59]

    rest is same as scan 1.20!!

1.6 Top Fidelity Select scan by 6 mo ROC:

    [favorites list = 26]

    rest is same as scan 1.3 !!

1.7 Top ETF Commodity scan by 6 mo ROC:

    [favorites list = 47]

    rest is same as scan 1.3 !!

1.8 Top Foreign ETF scan by 6 mo ROC:

   [favorites list = 43]

 rest is same as scan 1.3 !!

1.9 Scan for 12 mo highs in ETFs:

   [[favorites list = 1] or [favorites list = 191] or favorites list = 47]]

   and [todays daily close > 1 day ago max(253,daily high)]

2.0 Scan for 3 mo highs in ETFs:

   [[favorites list = 1] or [favorites list = 191] or [favorites list = 47]]

   and [todays daily close > 1 day ago max(66,daily high)]

2.1 Breakout Scan for ETFs"

   [[favorites list = 1] or [favorites list = 191] or [favoriteslist = 47]]

   and [daily close > 23 days ago max(104,daily high)]

   and [1 day ago max 21,daily high) < 23 days ago max(104,daily high)]

2.2 Top Industry Scan by 6 mo ROC:

   [favorites list = 40]

 rest is same as in scan 1.3 !!

2.3 scan for new 12 mo highs in Industries:

[favoriteslist = 40]

rest is same as in scan 1.9 !!

3.0 Top Stocks scan :

[[group is SP500] or [group is SP400] or [group is SP600] or

[group is DOW30] or [group is NASDAQ100]]

and daily PPO line(12,26,9,daily close) >= 0]

and [daily RSI(14) >= 50]

and [SCTR >= 60]

and [daily close > daily sma(200,daily close)]

and [daily sma(2,daily close) > daily ema(25,daily close)]

and [daily sma(2,daily close) > daily Upper Kelt Chan(105,3.0,30)]

and [daily upper Kelt Chan(105,3.0,30) >= daily Ichimoku Cloud Top(9,26,52)]

and [ema(25,daily close) >= ema(105,daily close)]

and [ema(105,daily close) >= sma(200,daily close)]

and [weekly PPO line(1,5,0) > 0]

and [weekly PPO line(5,13,0) > 0]

and [weekly PPO line(21,34,0) > 0]

and [weekly Slope(25) > 0]

and [weekly ROC(25) >= 10]

and [weekly ROC(12) >= 5]

and [weekly ROC(4) >= 1.66]

and weekly ROC(1) >= 0]

and [market cap >= 6,500]

and [daily sma(66,daily close) >= 7.50]

and [daily sma(66,daily volume) >= 400,000]

Rank by [weekly ROC(25)]

3.1 Top Stock scan for market cap < 6,500:

same as scan 3.0 except

and [market cap < 6,500]

and [market cap >= 500]

and sma(66,daily close) >= 5.50]

and [sma(66,daily volume) >= 300,000]

3.2 Top Stock scan for Stocks in a SECTOR:

same as scan 3.0 except you include [group is TechnologySector] beneath [[group is SP500] and [group is SP400] etc.

3.2 Scan for 12 mo high in stocks:

group is same as in scan 3.0

and [todays close > 1 day ago max(253,daily high)]

and [market cap >= 500]

and [sma(66,daily close) >= 5.50]

and [sma(66,daily volume) >= 300,000]

3.3 Scan for 3 mo high in stocks:

group is same as in scan 3.0

and [todays close > 1 day ago max(66,daily high)]

and [market cap >= 500]

and [sma(66,daily close) >= 5.50]

and [sma(66,daily volume) >= 300,000

3.4 Early Entry scan for stocks:

group is same as in scan 3.0

and [todays sma(2,daily close) x todays upper Kelt Chan(105,3.0,30)]

and [[44 days ago sma(2,daily close) < 44 days ago lower Kelt Chan(105,3.0,30)]

or [33 days ago sma(2,daily close) < 33 days ago lower Kelt Chan(105,3.0,30)]

or [22 days ago sma(2,daily close) < 22 days ago lower Kelt Chan(105,3.0,30)]

or [11 days ago sma(2,daily close) < 11 days ago lower Kelt Chan(105,3.0,30)]

and [[market cap >= 500]

and [sma(50,dail close) >= 5.50]

and [sma(50,daily volume) >= 300,00]

3.50 Gap up scan for stocks:

group is same as scan 3.0

and [pctchange(1,daily close) >= 8]

and [todays daily low > 1 day ago daily high*1.01]

and [daily volume >= daily sma(50,daily volume)*0.75]

and [daily sma(2,daily close) > daily upper Kelt Chan(105,3.0,30)]

and [sma(50,daily close) >= 5.50]

and sma(50,daily volume >= 300,000]

and [market cap >= 500]

3.60 Breakout Scan for Stocks:

same group as 3.0

and [[daily close > 23 days ago max(104,daily high)]

and 1 day ago daily max(21,daily high) < 23 days ago max(104,daily high)]

and [market cap >= 500]

and [todays sma(50,daily volume) >= 300,000]

and [sma(50,daily close) >= 5.50]

2.0 PullBack scan for stocks, breakouts and gaps up

[[group is sp500] or [group is sp400] or [group is sp600] or [group

is NASDAQ100] or [group is DOW30] or [favorites list = 207] or

[favorites list = 181]]

and [daily close <= daily ema(14,daily close)]

and [daily close >= daily sma(65,daily close)]

and [daily max(22,daily high) >= todays daily close*0.045]

and [daily max(22,SCTR) >= 75]

and [daily max(22,RSI(14)) >= 60

and [daily close <= daily ema(5,daily close)]

and [daily low < 1 day ago daily low]

and [1 day ago daily low < 2 days ago daily low]

and [2 days ago daily low < 3 days ago daily low]

and [3 days ago daily low < 4 days ago daily low]

and [market cap >= 500]

and [sma(50,daily close) >= 5.50]

and [sma(50,daily volume >= 300,000

and [PE Ratio < 400]

3.10 Pullback Stocks with a Reversal scan:

[favorites list = 102]

and [todays daily high >= 1 day ago daily high]

and [1 day ago daily high < 2 days ago daily high]

and[2 days ago daily high < 3 days ago daily high]

and [todays high > todays sma(5,daily close)]

4.0 Exit scan for trades in my investment and trading accounts:

[[favorites list = 92] or [favorites list = 223]]

and [[[daily sma(2, RSI(14)) < 40]

and [daily sma(2,daily close) < daily sma(50,daily close)]]

or [[daily sma(2,daily close < daily upper Kelt Chan(105,3.0,30)]

and [daily sma(2,RSI(14)) < 40]]

or [daily sma(2,ROC(50)) < 3.50]

or [[weekly PPO line(1,5,0) < 0]

or [weekly PPO line(5,13,0) < 0]

or [weekly PPO line(21,34,0) < 0]]]

Note: the weekly ROC values are based on the following:

1. the average yearly return for Bonds based on the Barclays US aggregate bond indesis 4%

2. the average yearly return for the SP500 is between 9 and 10%

3. For stocks I want a min average yearly return that is double that of the SP 500 or 20%

4. for Industries and etf Sub sectors I want a min average yearly return of 15%

5. for Sectors, Blend etfs, and market cap and Style etfs and I want a min average yearly return above 5%

Chapter 11. Determining Market Tops and Market Bottoms

It is important to be able to judge when the "market" is topping or bottoming. This can be done with classical technical analysis where from a market top you get a series of lower highs and lower lows, or from a market bottom you get a series of higher lows and higher highs, however this trend change indicator lags a bit.

For determining market tops the indicators I have found most useful are:

1.the relative strength ratio of the weekly XLK:SPY. XLK can can start underperforming SPY on the weekly relative strength chart months before a market top, and this serves a a warning to start looking at other indicators. the daily chart for XLY: XLP can also confirm a market top

2. The relative strength ratio of the weekly XLY:XLP. This is the most important chart to look at for determining a market top and when consumer discretionary starts underperforming consumer staples you are at a market top.

3. You now try to confirm the weekly XLY:XLP signal by looking for "divergences" on the daily charts of SPY.

a. the daily daily PPO line(12,26,9) will start sloping down.

b. the Daily RSI(14) will start sloping down

c. the SCTR will start sloping down

and all these three occur while the candlestick price pattern is still sloping up.

4. Drawing trend lines on the cumulative $NYAD(NYSE advance - decline line)

5. When the weekly ROC(12,SPY)(the 12 week rate of change for SPY crosses below -1.50 you are at a market top

6. when the weekly 2 yr Rate of Change for SPY(weekly ROC(104,SPY) crosses above 60% this is unsustainable and you are at or near a market top.

5. Contrary Sentiment indicators can indicate a top: the 5 day sma of the $CPCE(the CBOE options equity put/call ratio falls below 0.55 indicating an excess of optimism in the markets

To hedge a portfolio in a bearish market regime you must be able to identify or come close to identifying the "market bottom" . This can be done visually if you are an experienced technical analyst. In the recent 2025 market bottom in April there were very long hollow candlesticks with higher highs and huge volumes, however most of the times its best to rely on market bottom indicators.

1. The relative strength of the weekly XLK:SPY and XLY:XLP. Here the market bottom is indicated when they bottom out below the weekly sma(30) and start turning up

2. the Pring bottom fisher indicator(!PRBFISH). This indicator has good correlation to the actual bottom in bearish market regimes in SPY. When is falls below -30 and peaks you are at or near a market bottom.

weekly chart with 8 yr timespan

!PRBFISH with solid line

horizontal line at - 30

3. Market bottom with weekly CCI(35)

weekly chart with 8 yr time span

weekly Candlestick chart for SPY weekly

weekly CCI(35) below

when the weekly CCI(35) falls below -100 and peaks you are at or near a market bottom

4.. Market Bottom with weekly PPO(12,26,9) below 0

weekly chart with 8 y r time span

weekly candlestick chart for SPY

weekly PPO(12,26,9) below with horizontal line at 0

when the weekly PPO falls below 0 and peaks you are at or near a market bottom

5. Market Bottom with daily Swenlin golden cross chart !GCISPX

8 yr time span with daily !GCISPX (Swenlin indicator) with horizontal line at 37. When the !GCISPX(percent of stocks in SP500 whose 50 day sma is below the 200 day sma(golden cross) falls below 37% and forms a peak you are at or near a market bottom.

6. Market bottom with $NYHLDJ(NYSE New Highs - New Lows-Dow Jones)(breadth)

8 yr weekly chart weekly $NYHLDJ with horizontal line at -600

price below with SPY candlestick chart

when the $NYHLDJ falls below - 600 and peaks you are at or near a market bottom

7. Market bottom with $SPX200R (market breadth)

8 yr weekly chart weekly $SPXA200R as solid line with horizontal lines at 80%,50% and 25%. When the $SPXA200R(% of stocks in SP500 above its 200 day moving average) falls below 25% and peaks you are at or near a market bottom.

8. Market bottom with $BPSPX(market breadth)

daily chart with 2yr time span and solid line price representation. When th $BPSPX falls below 30 and peaks you are at or near a market bottom. This represent the percentage of stocks in SP500 with point and figure buy signals.

9. market bottoms with weekly ROC(17) for SPY

when the Wkly ROC(17) for Spy crosses below -1.50 and starts reversing from a bottom peak you are at the market bottom.

1..Market Tops with weekly ROC(12) for SPY

weekly Chart with 6 yr time span

weekly $SPX price represented by solid line

weekly ROC(11) with horizontal line at -1.50, and +1.50

when the weekly ROC(12) falls below -1.50 and peaks you are at or near a market bottom.

This is my favorite market top chart

2. market Tops with XLK:SPY or XLY:XLP

your are near a market top when when the weekly sma(2,XLK:SPY) line starts turning down and crosses below the 35 week sma.

Use these charts to help you identify the market bottom. At or near a market bottom you use all your cash to buy SPY and you ride the uptrend that eventually follows. You don't even need to identify the actual market bottom to come out ahead. If the market drops 15% you reinvest 25% of your money in SPY. If it drops 20% you reinvest another 25 % in SPY. If it drop 25% you reinvest another 25% in SPY, and if it drops 30% you reinvest the final 25 % in SPY

Chapter 12.   Interest Rates and US dollar

   Professional investors and traders pay an extraordinary amount of attention to when the Fed is starting a series of interest rate cuts, or a series of interest hikes. The amount of time and energy they devout to deciphering "Fed Speak" is unbelievable, and the Fed has a habit of not showing its hand until the last moment when the final economic reports on the Economic calendar are in. I personally think it borders on hysteria but thats the way it is.

   When a cycle of interest rate cuts starts it raises the value of stocks and stimulates the entire economy by reducing the interest rates for corporations that are capital intensive(need to borrow large amounts of capital(money) pay to accomplish their business an growth needs). It also allows consumers to borrow at lower costs to finance purchases of a home or automobile etc. which further stimulates the economy. It stimulates the financial sector because banks do more business lending due to the lower rates, and asset managers and investment services do more business because the stock market usually rises with lower rates and investors are more bullish and invest and trade more.

   The effect of lowering interest rates on the current value of a stock is mathematical. The current value of a stock is the perception of its future cash flows discounted to the present. I dont know all the math but essentially when interest rates are lower the discounted value is higher and when interest rates rise the discounted value is lower. Thus the mere lowering of interest rates increases the value of all stocks.

Industries and Sectors that tend to rise with interest rate cuts:

1. Small and Mid cap stocks (capital intensive)

2. Financials (XLF,KBE,KRE, Investment Services,Banks,Mortgage REITS)

3.Real Estate(XLRE) especially real estate investment trusts (capital intensive)

4. Utilities(XLB) (capital intensive)

5. Consumer Discretionary(investor sentiment is bullish and they buy more things they want)

6. Industrials(XLI)(economy expands with lower intrest rates)

7. Materials(XLB) with lower interest rates the dollar weakens and this raises the price of materials, as does the the increase in demand from the booming economy

8. Technology(XLK) (capital intensive)

9. Home Construction(ITB) (lower mortgage rates)

10. Home Improovements(HD,Low)

11. Building Materials

12. Automobiles and Auto Parts

13. Renewable Energy Stocks (capital intensive)

14. Mortgage REITS

15. Precious Metals(lower interest rates decrease the strength of the dollar)

16. Real Estate Reits, Real EState Specialty Reits, Real Estate Development(capital intensive)

17. Residential and Hotel Reits

note REITS stand for Real Estate Investment Trusts

18. Recreational Services

When an interest rate hike cycle starts all the above will be affected negatively as many are capital intensive and the cost of capital increases. Economic activity will tend to gradually tighten and shrink and the stock market will start falling. Treasury bonds will fall in value and their yields will increase. As I have watched the market over time I can't help notice how the market responds to every economic(macro) input from he economic calendar. It almost appears that each macro input is fed into a computer program that analyses it for the effect it will have on stocks, and that this program then calculates the stock equity exposure one should have in a portfolio, and that the major financial institutions then adjust their equity exposure to meet the recommended level. I'm certain this is going on but such programs are not available to the individual investor. However the individual investor can to some extent mimic the above by knowing the state of the market regime and the permission to trade long scan, and adjust their trading and investing activity accordingly.

The Us Dollar:

Fluctuations in the value of the US Dollar can have significant effects on certain industries and foreign markets.

When the US dollar falls in value it cost more in dollars to buy physical assets like materials: gold, silver, steel , copper, platinum,chemicals, raw materials,live stock, agricultural products etc. so all these metals will rise in value and so will the mining companies that produce them, and the materials Sectoir , XLB will also rise in value. And when the US dollar rises in value, all the above will cost less to purchse ant their price will fall in value.

The same thing occurs with the stocks and currency fo Foreign Markets. When the dollar falls it costs more dollars to buy foreign stocks and thus in dollar terms their price will rise. When the dollar rises it costs less dollars to buy foreign stocks and thus their price will fall.

The value of the dollar is a function of the real interest rate on US Bonds(interest rate - inflation rate = real interest rate), the strength and stability of the US govt and economy, and the perception of the US as a stable democracy, and the amount of debt the country carries.

Gold is thought of as a safe haven, and most of the time it is. Its value is determined by several factors:

1. the stability and state of the "market(spy)"

2. the marco enviornment of the entire world(eg. wars, financial crises, Catastrophies

3. the VIx

4. the amount of gold purchased by "Sovereign Wealth Funds)

5. rising or falling interest rates. Rising interest rates strengthen the dollar, and the price of gold is always stated in dollars,so with rising interest rates gold will fall in price, and investors will switch to bonds from gold because of the rising interest rates and return they can get from bonds.

falling interest rates will cause the price of gold to rise as it weakens the dollar, and the return on bonds is less attractive.

So for gold to prosper as a safe haven interest rates need to be falling, the strength of the dollar needs to fall, and there should be no precipitous falls in the price of the SP500 which could generate huge algorithmic selling of all stocks and etfs in a portfolio including gold. This is what happened in March of 2026. Interest rates started rising, the dollar started rising, and there was as sudden precipitous drop in the "market" causing algorithmic selling across the board.

Chapter 13.   Dealing with taxes on capital gains, interest and dividends in your non-IRA investment and trading accounts.

In your IRAs you don't have to worry about capital gains, interest or dividends. as they ae not taxed. When you make the yearly required minimum distribution after you retire, this is taxed as income.

In your non-IRA investment and trading accounts you must have a mechanism of dealing with capital gains, interest and dividends otherwise at the end of the year you could be in for a big surprise for how much you owe on them in income tax, and have to come up with large sums of money to pay your taxes. This could do you in if you don't plan for it.

The way I have found to deal with this problem is as follows. I have found that if I use the percentage of tax I paid in the last year (total taxes paid federal and state) / my total income for the year) and apply that percentage to the sum of my total capital gains, interest and dividends for the current year that brings me pretty close to what I need to set aside for taxes on my dividends, interest and capital gains. Don't be concerned about the tax on capital gains and qualified dividends being less than the tax on income. This is becoming a fallacy with the addition of the Obamacare tax and the alternative minimum tax raising the tax on those items to close to the tax on income.

To find the amount of interest, dividends and capital gains I have generated in a quarter in my Fidelity accounts I log into Fidelity and go the upper left hand corner "Accounts and Trades" click on it and go down to "Tax Forms and information" and click on that. That brings up several choices. Choose "View your Year- to-Date Tax activity" and that will bring up the current interest, dividends and capital gains or losses that you have generated on each of your non IRA investment accounts and trading accounts. You do this on the last day of a quarter in March, June, Sept, and December. You now calculate the total amount of interest, dividends and capital gains from each of these accounts. You take this total and multiply it by the percentage of your income that you pay in taxes that you calculated above. This is the amount you must set aside this quarter in a money market fund to pay the taxes that your investments have generated. Let's say the total tax rate on your income comes to comes to 25%, and 80% of this is for federal taxes and 20% of this is for state taxes. If instead of capital gains you have capital losses in a quarter you can use those losses to offset capital gains in one of the other quarters. Thus, you must set aside 25% of all interest, dividends and net capital gains for taxes at least on a quarterly basis. If you don't do this you could be in for a nasty surprise at years end and have to come up with a lot of cash. I personally do this on a monthly basis.